Best Mates

Helen Orme

Street**Wise**

Best Mates
by Helen Orme

Published by Ransom Publishing Ltd.
Radley House, 8 St. Cross Road, Winchester, Hampshire SO23 9HX, UK
www.ransom.co.uk

ISBN   978 184167 345 5
First published in 2014

Copyright © 2014 Ransom Publishing Ltd.
Text copyright © 2014 Helen Orme
Cover photograph copyright © natenn.

A CIP catalogue record of this book is available from the British Library.

All rights reserved. No part of this publication may be reproduced, stored in a retrieval system, or transmitted, in any form or by any means, electronic, mechanical, photocopying, recording or otherwise, without the prior permission of the publishers.

The right of Helen Orme to be identified as the author of this Work has been asserted by her in accordance with sections 77 and 78 of the Copyright, Design and Patents Act 1988.

CONTENTS

1	At the Bus Stop	7
2	Friday Night	10
3	He Couldn't Refuse	15
4	In Town	20
5	Feeling Good	24
	Questions on the Story	27
	Discussion Points	30
	Activities	33

ONE
At the Bus Stop

Gary Stone saw Rick and Pete most days. The school bus picked them up from the village, and by eight o'clock there was always quite a crowd hanging around the bus stop.

It was a difficult time of day for Gary.

Rick and Pete were best mates, and they weren't interested in talking to him.

All of the rest were girls, and they didn't want to talk to Gary either.

Gary tried to get to the bus stop as late as possible. Once, he had missed the bus, and it was a very long walk to the school!

*****

One Friday, Pete wasn't at the bus stop. One of the girls asked Rick where he was.

'Haven't you heard? He's been suspended.'

'What for?'

'He mouthed off Roberts. Said a few naughty words.'

Mr Roberts was the deputy head. He was a tough character.

Gary wished he was brave enough to tell him what he thought of him!

TWO

Friday Night

None of Gary's friends went to his school.

They all lived in a town five miles away.

Gary's family had moved from the town

to the village just before he started at

secondary school, and he was then in a

different catchment area.

He had never really liked the school he was at.

*****

Most Friday evenings, Gary went into town to see his best mate, Jason.

The last bus back to the village was at 10 o'clock. If he missed it, it was either a long walk home in the dark or a phone

call to Mum – and she wasn't pleased when that happened!

That night he had been in time for the bus. He got off at the village green and headed for home.

In the dark ahead he saw two people. They heard Gary's footsteps and stopped and looked around.

Gary started to feel nervous.

He saw it was Rick and Pete.

They were both smoking.

THREE

He Couldn't Refuse

'If it isn't Gary Stone!'

That was Rick.

Was he being friendly – or threatening?

Gary couldn't tell.

But he couldn't hang back, now they

had seen him.

'Wanna ciggie, Gary?'

Gary definitely didn't. He didn't smoke, and wasn't going to start.

But they were watching him.

He didn't think he could really refuse.

He took the cigarette and let Rick light it for him.

He took a puff.

It tasted really disgusting. He tried

hard not to show it, though.

He walked along with them for a little way, then turned for home. He wanted to get away from them as soon as he could, so he could ditch the cigarette without them seeing.

*****

As soon as he got in, he was in trouble. His mum sniffed at him as he walked past.

'Gary, you've been smoking! I can smell it on your breath!'

Oh no! How was he going to talk himself out of this one?

FOUR

In Town

The next Friday, Gary was sitting on the bus heading into town. He was off to see Jason, as usual.

Then he got a text.

CANT C U TONITE. THROWING UP EVERYWHERE. SORRY MATE. JASE.

What was he going to do? He was almost in town.

There was no point in getting off and walking home.

There wasn't another bus until much later.

*****

He got off at the bus station and mooched along to the cinema, to see if

anything decent was on.

Typical. Some stupid movie about a load of cuddly toys coming to life, with queues of adults lining up to see it.

He wandered back to the bus station.

There, sitting in one of the shelters, were Rick and Pete. They must have come in to town on an earlier bus.

'What ya doing here then, Gary? Fancy a drink, mate?'

Gary sat down with them.

Pete opened a can and passed it over.

Gary drank quite a lot before he realised it was cider, and quite strong.

FIVE
Feeling Good

Gary began to feel good.

Rick and Pete treated him like a mate.

They'd never done that before.

They wandered round the town. It began to drizzle, but they didn't care.

They wandered down a street where there were roadworks. There were traffic cones around a raised manhole cover. Rick picked one up and put it on his head.

Soon they were laughing and chucking the cones all over the place.

*****

It happened so suddenly. There was a roar, and a motor-bike turned the corner.

It hit the raised manhole cover.

The bike skidded on the slippery road.

The rider fell off and slammed into a wall.

'Come on, out of here!'

That was Rick.

He and Pete ran off.

But Gary couldn't. The rider needed help.

He got out his phone to call an ambulance.

It was then that he saw the CCTV camera pointing straight at him.

Questions on the Story

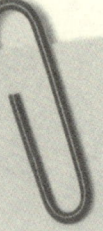

- What was Gary's main problem?

- Why did Gary have a difficult time at the bus stop?

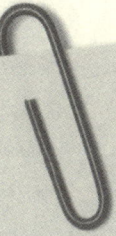

- Why did Gary feel good at the start of Chapter Five?

Think of two reasons.

> # Discussion Points

- Why didn't Gary refuse the cigarette?

- At the end of the story, why didn't Gary run off with the others? What does that tell us about Gary?

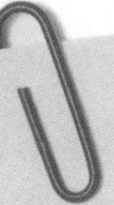

- Have you ever felt pressure from friends to do something you didn't want to do?

 How did you handle it?

Activities

- *'Gary, you've been smoking! I can smell it on your breath!'*

Continue the conversation.